Suddenly Your World Falls Apart

A Guide to Grieving Well

by

Nancy Markworth Brown

Suddenly – Your World Falls Apart
by Nancy Markworth Brown

Printed in the United States of America

ISBN-13: 978-1-60034-908-9
IBSN-10: 1-60034-908-0

www.xulonpress.com

Dedicated to: Milt, Robert, and Dennis
Also my writer-friends: Margaret, Sharon,
Carol, Chawna, Bill, Cheryl, and Jonathan

Table of Contents

Introduction.. vii

Chapter One—
    Suddenly 11
    What Do I Do After the Funeral?...........................12
    Brave Little Steps...15
    Workbook – Chapter One 18

Chapter Two—
    Rays of Hope...21
    Stages and Tasks of Grief.....................................22
    Workbook – Chapter Two 31

Chapter Three—
    What if … 33
    The Nagging "If Onlys".......................................34
    Workbook – Chapter Three....................................37

Chapter Four—
    Burying Grief or Walking Through It 41
    Your Pathway to Healing 43
    Workbook – Chapter Four.....................................48

Chapter Five—
    Crazy Anniversaries 51
    Memories that Heal 52
    Workbook – Chapter Five 56

Chapter Six—
    Widowhood—the Club You Didn't Want
        to Join 59
    Workbook – Chapter Six 65

Chapter Seven—
    Wishing for What Might Have Been 67
    The "Saint" Issue 70
    Workbook – Chapter Seven 72

Chapter Eight—
    Sharing Our Stories, Healing Our Souls 75
    Workbook – Chapter 82

Chapter Nine—
    How Do I Go On? 85
    Making Progress 87
    Workbook – Chapter Nine 91

Chapter Ten—
    What is My Reason for Living? What is My
        Passion? 93
    The Blessed Hope 99
    Workbook – Chapter Ten 101

Recommended Reading 103

Introduction

Welcome, I am glad you are here!
I'm not glad you are grieving, but I am glad you are exploring ways to walk through the valley of grief and loss.

I don't know whether you have picked up this book to read, or if you are in a Grief Support group with others. Either way, I want to encourage you that there is *life after grief*.

Grief is a natural part of life. You cannot rush its healing process. Healing is a foreseeable goal, and God is terribly concerned about your wellbeing. Burying the pain is only to face it later. Grief can lead you into senseless depression, or it can bring you into a time of faith and hope—into new life. Choose to "grieve well" and you will be on the path to wholeness.

If you have lost a spouse or someone very dear to you and your grief seems almost insurmountable, this book is for you. I will share my experience of devastating losses. I know how sudden and final the death of a beloved one feels; death is sudden, even if you've expected it for a while.

I lost two husbands to sudden heart attacks. "Where is my hope now?" I asked God. I waited, wept, and listened. Do you know what? —He showed me! I pray that I will also be able to show you a path that I'd like to describe as "joy in the mourning." Grieve well and you will experience this.

The Workbook pages are at the end of each chapter. If you are doing this with a group, or a friend, one of you could facilitate, or you could take turns.

I also recommend sharing and praying for each another's prayer requests. This will help foster intimacy and this is what you need now. Make this be a safe place by keeping everything confidential. We are most vulnerable when we share innermost feelings.

I suggest using a covenant rule such as the one provided below, so that everyone will understand what is expected. If new members visit or join, be sure this covenant is read and understood.

> "We, the members of (blank) Church will meet each (time and day) to share and pray together. We agree to listen to our fellow members, not to give advice (unless asked for, and then sparingly.) We also agree not to dominate the group allowing all members to share if they wish. We believe the truth that all things shared in the group, should stay confidential in the group. We'll allow the group leader to facilitate and keep things running smoothly."
>
> Signed_____

This book will help you do the hard work of grieving well, but it happens by taking on the process slowly, bravely, and gently—with the compassionate help of our Savior. I have heard it said, "Shared burdens are halved; shared joys are multiplied." If you go through the book attentive to the love and whispers of God, openly reflective, you'll see God's light shining in the darkness. The Workbook pages are here for you to experience God's nearness. Take your time; please don't hurry. Alone or as a group, spending time praying the passages suggested will sharpen anew the knowledge of God's tremendous care for you. My hope is that the love of our dear Savior Jesus will strengthen and fill you with deep and great joy.

Chapter One

Suddenly

Who would have guessed that my husband, Milt, an avid biker, a busy pastor in a large church, with so much to live for, would die?

Before that, my life was wonderful. I felt so secure in my marriage. Milt had been crazy about me and I about him. We were best friends, partners in our daily lives, in ministry, and in raising our family. Our first priority was God and loving Him, then each other. We had thirty-three wonderful years together—the kind of marriage our friends and children admired. Then suddenly, it was over!

I kissed Milt goodbye that morning; it was an ordinary, beautiful fall day. If I had known it was our last one together, I would have clung to him longer, kissed him more deeply and told him, as I often did, how much I loved him. But I thought we had lots of days ahead of us and plenty of time to do that. How wrong I was.

That night as I was preparing supper, I heard the sound of his bicycle falling down on the porch where he usually kept it. I assumed it had just slipped out of his grasp. Regardless, I went to help him. Then I saw that his body was lying across the door. Alarmed, I went around through the garage to get to his side and saw that his face looked ghostly pale. His body was shaking. I wanted so badly to hold him but, instead, needed to get help for him. Things looked bad.

Something came over me, a robotic-like consciousness of shock. Everything became foggy from the 911 call and neighbors coming, to the paramedics arriving. I kept saying, "Milt, don't leave me!" But inside myself, my thoughts were frantically pulsing—"He's going to be okay, right? This isn't happening! This is just a test, isn't it God?"

The end result was that my husband never revived and we never said goodbye.

A part of me died with him. Another part disbelieved it. I walked around in a fog. People said things to me; I shook hands, and did what had to be done. Perhaps you understand this state, if you have picked up this book to read because you've lost a dear one.

Knowing that Milt was with the Lord gave some comfort. But the loss was so great. At first his death didn't seem real; it was like a nightmare that I hoped to wake up from. Whenever the reality of his death struck again, I was devastated.

The fabric of my wonderful life was torn apart never to be the same again. But I am happy to say that the fabric has been mended and patched, like a beautiful quilt. Things are good again. It's true my life will never be as it was with Milt. I still miss him, but I focus now on the privilege it was to know and love him.

May I share my grief journey and what I learned along the way?

What Do I Do After The Funeral?

I watched as Milt's sister, Mavis, and her husband Dave drove away. An emptiness and blackness descended. I felt so terribly alone. They had stayed with me until after the funeral. They had helped me in so many ways: with funeral plans, and finances, which I had never had the heart for. Their company had given me a reason to get up in the morning. It was comforting to have someone in the house with me. Now I was all by myself, never having lived alone.

I'd gone from my parents' home to my first teaching job in St. Louis, renting a room at Mrs. Ruth's, a lady from my church.

Soon I was married and had a houseful of children. One by one they moved away to start their own lives. They were doing well. My husband and I were looking forward to our retirement together. We had dreams and plans for travel and short-term mission work. I was fifty-six and in good health, but now life seemed empty and bleak because Milt was gone.

We had enjoyed a sweet and mellow rhythm to our life. God first. Teamwork, play, and fun. We enjoyed eating out at restaurants as well as trying out new ways to cook healthy food in our cozy kitchen. Life was good; we were together. We exercised daily and prayed together. Best of all, we shared sunrises and end-of-the-day thoughts. Hugs, kisses, and encouragement were frequent. We were best friends and lovers.

After his passing, I felt lopsided, a boat without a rudder, a blank person with a broken heart. I was a big wound dripping blood, my life oozing away. I wanted to die. Taking my life was no option, but I thought about it for the first time in my life.

Questions plagued me. Why God? Why now when I need him so? Why was there so little warning? How does anyone get through this?

Where could I go for answers to my questions? Not one friend my age had gone through this yet. When I tried talking to the older widows, they were full of platitudes. For most of them it had been years and they were from a generation that had stifled feelings until they couldn't feel anymore.

Could I do that? I didn't think so. I needed to find someone to talk to, anyone who had recently gone through this and managed to keep functioning. How had they put one foot in front of the other and made a new beginning in life? I needed help.

I wondered if a small support group would help me. I had been told about one that met at the hospital where Milt died; they met there once a month. I had put off going to it. It was hard to think about going to that place where my world collapsed. But soon the dinner invitations and phone calls eased off and my friends went on with their own lives. Even my children, though they missed their dad, didn't have the daily relationship I had had with him. They seemed to be adjusting to his absence much better than I. If they were grieving, they were doing it in private.

Finally, I went. My need for help was strong enough to get me there, but my first experience with the group was a disaster. I shared my story about how Milt had died. I explained that as painful as that had been, I was having trouble with my youngest son who had just returned from a semester overseas. No doubt acting out his grief, he hardly spoke to me. I had expected he would be a comfort and company for me. The silence was hard to bear and worse than being alone.

When I confided this, a one-time participant gave me some harsh advice and no one stopped her. She said I should kick him out. I knew that was not the answer. My son had just lost his father and he was dealing with his anger and grief badly. To force him to leave when he was vulnerable, seemed unthinkable. I was angry at that bad advice and that no one had disagreed with her. I planned to never come back to the group. Then three months later, I found the strength to go back, if nothing else to tell them that this advice had upset me. When I told them, they apologized and asked for my forgiveness. Of course, I did forgive them. I learned that there were group rules that had not been read that first time.

I know now that it's very important to listen, listen, and listen some more, to a grieving person. Sharing your own experience is good, but you should not tell people what to do. They need, more than anything else, to talk about their experience.

Then I was glad that I returned to the group. While involved with these dear people, I tried to learn what helps a grieving person and what doesn't. This group soon became a source of growth to me. I was comforted to hear that some who were farther along in the grief process were adjusting better to their loss. It gave me hope.

The benefit of a group, if functioning properly, is that you see that others have feelings similar to yours. In our society, a grieving person can feel like a misfit. Many have told me that they feel crazy and strange. Am I normal? This is a question one often asks.

During these days of healing, I talked to counselors, a therapist, friends, and neighbors. I wrote in my journal, prayed and read all the books I could find about bereavement. I kept busy.

A year and a half later, I still didn't feel as healed as I thought I should be. A grief support weekend put on by a Christian-based organization helped me bit more.

Brave Little Steps

I began to trust in God's direction more hopefully. "Maybe I've made some progress," I wrote in my journal one day.

I found an easy exercise that helped me a great deal: I would recall special moments, one each day, when I felt the closest to the Lord. I sensed God was asking me to find a surprise in each day. I did. Even little ones like an unexpected phone call, helped. I tried to walk through my grief, and not stuff my feelings. I looked to God in the midst of my pain. This was a decision and it brought me hope.

I realized that grief was work and it was a process. I knew about the stages of grief, and wanted to charge through them, checking off one at a time: shock, anger, etc. It didn't happen like I hoped because sometimes I'd revisit a place I had been a month ago. I'd thought I was all finished with that one and it surprised me. Yet each time that happened, looking back I could see some healing. I just had to keep going on.

Holidays were hard. I found that *un-holidays* were also hard, when a pleasant memory of my beloved would occur. Something would trigger it—a smell, a place, almost anything could pop up to remind me of him. Then the finality of "never again" would surface and cause the tears to flow. Tears were good but they didn't always come at convenient times.

The hardest thing for me was feeling alienation from God. At a time when I thought God would be close to me, He seemed to be hiding His face. Where was He in my blackest hour when everything seemed senseless?

Much later I realized He had been near me all the time, hidden from my sight by my shock and despair. Great psychic pain had twisted my perspective. I was like Mary Magdalene who saw Jesus in the garden and didn't recognize Him.

Since I am a person who deeply loves God, I was surprised at what I thought was His "treatment" of me. I thought there would be an explanation or revelation as to why a seemingly healthy man who did so much good, would have to die so young. My questions received no answers. I could not "hear" them anyway.

Technically, I knew anger was a legitimate stage of grief. Mine was directed toward God because I needed someone to blame. Then I'd feel guilty about my anger and my blaming Him. I still believed there was a God, but doubted His goodness. Some days I waited for Him to "zap" me. That would be all right with me. I didn't care.

It is so wonderful that God isn't like us. He doesn't return our anger, but waits for us to recover a bit, lick our wounds and return to Him. And when I did return, I received a fervent and loving homecoming from my Beloved Lord.

Later I remembered those feelings of distrust and blame when I read a quote by Elie Wiesel. This man wrote that he was angry with God because the holocaust took away many of his loved ones. He said something like this, "I missed God so much that I went back to believing in Him again."

I felt the same way. I couldn't live without God. I, too, had missed Him too much!

Workbook – Chapter One

Death may have struck suddenly. If so, you may not have ever had time to think about what would ensue immediately after: the funeral, the change in lifestyle, the financial matters, etc. There are just so many implications of the loss you are now faced with. How do you cope? How do you go forward?

Since my husband had always been healthy, I thought these things were years away. I have talked with others who lived in the denial of an impending death, even when the spouse had a terminal illness. These deaths also had a feeling of suddenness, and a survivor must immediately take practical and unwanted steps.

Each person has a unique way of coping with disappointment and loss. Jesus, when he lived on the earth, had plenty of those experiences. This is amazing considering He was fully God. He was just as human as we are.

Let's listen in on a day in the synagogue in Nazareth, when Jesus announced "his mission" when He quoted these words from

❖ Isaiah 61:1:
"The Spirit of the Lord is on me . . . To bind up the brokenhearted . . . to comfort all who mourn..."

Reflect on this verse.
Jesus knew what it was to suffer and grieve, having walked in our world. What are Jesus' promises to you in these words from Scripture?

_____

_____

_____

Read verse three:

❖ Isaiah 61:3:
". . . to bestow on them a crown of beauty instead of ashes, the oil of gladness instead of mourning, and a garment of praise instead of a spirit of despair."

What do you think Jesus might mean by *"beauty in the midst of ashes?"* Have you experienced anything good during this time of loss? What does this promise mean to you today?

What has been the oil of joy in your mourning?

_____

_____

_____

Have you been given a garment of praise? Can you praise God in the midst of grief for anything, even a small thing?

_____

_____

_____

Has your spirit of heaviness lifted for a while? What has helped?

_____

_____

_____

Chapter Two

Rays of Hope

One of the rays of hope came a year and a half after Milt died, when I met Robert Bortot. We met at a Christian Grief Weekend. I wondered how men deal with grief and as we began to speak about our losses, he impressed me with his devotion to his wife who'd had cancer. I thought he was a nice man, but was surprised when he phoned me and asked me to go to dinner. I was nervous about dating, but it was also fun and exciting. It felt good to be liked. But, I wasn't ready for anything but friendship. I couldn't fathom being in a serious relationship.

That night we talked and talked. We had so much in common, including writing, teaching and leading small groups. He had a wonderful laugh and the warmest hugs. He didn't overstep any boundaries and treated me respectfully. On the second date, he shared that he, too, was nervous and was glad that I appreciated 50s values. And on the third date, when he asked if he could go to church with me, I felt that God had led me to this friend.

We began to have all the classic symptoms that come with romance: trouble eating, sleeping, and daydreaming a lot. We wanted to be together all the time and finally we admitted to each other that we were in love. Gone was the deep loneliness. We could be so transparent with each other and share that we still missed our former spouses.

That was a huge blessing; he understood my loss and not be jealous of my past life.

At first my children had a hard time with this, but realized that loving Robert did not keep me from loving their dad. They grew to care for Robert and we enjoyed both sets of children and grandchildren. Life was full and rich again.

We founded New Morning Ministries, giving grief seminars and classes to help people to deal with grief and loss just as we had. More healing came from this. We were glad to give back what we had received.

There will always be rays of hope for you from God. The Scriptures say, "Draw near to God and He will draw near to you." Look for how He might minister to you. There will be occasions, persons, and places that He will use to reach out to you. "God–with-skin-on," is what I needed. And, I looked for the all those ways that God might use to help me.
Pay attention to how He brings opportunities across your path—keep your eyes and ears open. You can receive His comforting words, be prayed for, and soak in His healing presence. You'll need some rest and quiet, because grieving is emotionally draining and will wear you down.

Some of the ways God helped me, as I've mentioned earlier, were: a Grief Support Group, a Christian retreat for the bereaved, individual helpers and counselors, and books. I was able to glean a lot from what others had learned and experienced. The books that spoke about typical stages of grief helped me a lot. I realized this was a journey of uncharted territory.

Stages and Tasks of Grief
Death happens. In earlier times, people expected to live much shorter lives than we do these days. Often, babies lived

only a few days and mothers died during childbirth. With improved medical treatment, better food and exercise, longer life expectancy continues to rise. Yet we all know that death is inevitable and can take anyone at any time.

Since 1969, Elisabeth Kubler-Ross' book on stages of grief, "On Death and Dying," has been widely acclaimed. This book has helped many people to better understand and deal with death. Having worked in hospice care, Kubler-Ross wrote about what she saw and learned from her dying patients.

Her observations provide better understanding to a surviving loved one. While I differ with her philosophy on some other issues, her approach to the grief process was very helpful. Unfortunately, the term "stages" may make one feel that one can complete a stage and move on. Sometimes that's true, but you may go through a stage a second time. You may experience them in a different order. Be patient with yourself and you will progress.

Another writer, Janice Winchester Nadeau, has called what we experience, the "tasks of grief." (*Where Do I Go From Here?* Three one-hour cassettes published by Color Song Productions, P.O. Box 120321, St. Paul, MN 55112, 1993.)

Early in the grief process, one starts by accepting the fact that the loss has happened. I like the idea of the stages as being tasks, because they truly are work that must be done. Each task involves adjusting to the life-changing event in various ways. For example, we must fill out overwhelming amounts of paperwork for the financial part of the estate. That is part of the role transition that becomes immediate and practical in nature. In light of this, you may revisit earlier losses that reappear in our state of pain. Later on, such tasks are: to find meaning in the death of the loved one as an individual or with the family, and to complete the grief-work as much as possible at that time.

Kubler-Ross labels the first stage as "Denial and Isolation." But my first stage with Milt's death was Shock – and I remained in this state for a long time. His death was nearly impossible for me to believe. Shock remained though the denial stage. Remember that each person experiences it differently.

What is shock like? I walked around like a zombie for days. My brain felt fuzzy and I needed friends and family to tell me what to do next. I felt great, unrelenting pain. However lots of people's prayers had cushioned me for the days through the visitation, funeral, and burial. When those days of "shared mourning" ended, my sense of loss grew more intense. Had I experienced the pain all at once, I don't know how I would have managed. I felt physical symptoms that felt like broken glass stabbing into my skin. My head and neck both had tight bands around them.

When Robert died, my head reeled with the shock that this same tragedy could happen to me again, and so soon. In his case, I knew he had a heart condition when I married him. Because his doctor reported that he was doing fine, we were not concerned. We'd only been married for four years when he died. We were talking about our day that morning, when his face changed, head fell back against the couch. I desperately prayed that the man I loved so deeply would not die, but it happened. Again, I lost my partner in life and ministry. It was unbelievable. Because we had deeply shared our journey of healing, we were very close to one another. He had helped me heal from Milt's death and now he, too, was gone. I also knew how hard the grief process would be because I had gone through it before. I dreaded the work to come, anticipating the intensity of loss.

In this stage of foggy semi-consciousness, people would say, "If there is anything I can do, let me know." When someone is in shock, they don't know what to tell you. Even after the shock wore off, I appreciated it when someone would say something specific, "May I take you to lunch?" or even better, "Can I help you with anything?" Once someone asked, "Can I go on an errand with or for you?" I dreaded taking my husband's suits to the Good Will store and, so, I gave her the task. This dear friend came over and took care of this painful chore. When there is something you can't face, ask your friends.

The following are the stages of grief according to *On Death and Dying* by Elisabeth Kubler-Ross:

Stage 1: Denial and Isolation

Each morning when I woke up after Milt's death, I would say, "Did it really happen?" As the numbness wore off from the pill my doctor had given me to help me sleep, I was acutely aware it HAD happened. I kept this pattern up for months. The whole grieving process had unnerved me so much so that the reality of Milt's death seemed like a bad dream each morning until I was fully awake. Eventually I knew that his death was real. A friend said, "You are living my worst nightmare." "Mine too," I replied.

I know of introverts who have hidden in their houses, and friends had to literally drag them out. Time to reflect is fine; just don't isolate yourself. Friends need to help as much as you need to receive. Depression can get so much worse when you are alone constantly.

Extrovert that I am, I sought to be around people. But often, when one is grieving, people may withdraw from you because they cannot handle your loss. I heard from one person, "You're not fun any more, you're too sad."

Ouch! What am I supposed to do? Put on a happy face when I am dying inside? I appreciated friends who were just *there*. If I wanted to talk, they'd listen, and if I didn't, that was fine, too. That was wonderful to me.

"Role Changes" add to the crazed feeling. You are no longer a couple. When you find yourself in this new position, you see that you are living in *a couples' world* but you are no longer a part of it. That really hits you when you start feeling better; you're ready to socialize with your friends, couples, of course, and find you are not always included in "their" activities anymore.

Another change for me: I was no longer the pastor's wife at the church. Milt's salary ended a week after his death and I didn't know how I would manage financially. His position would soon be replaced with another man. More loss.

Losing my identity was part of the isolated feeling. I was still *me*. I was a mother, and a sister. But, alas, I was not a *wife* anymore. Now, I was "a widow," a widow with a big, black W on my chest.

Before my loss, I had thought I was a rather independent woman, but I found my interdependence with Milt to be a rich and important part of my life. How I missed it. How I missed *him*.

Stage 2: Anger

Early days of my anger stage were spent questioning why. The death of my husband seemed completely senseless. I was angry with myself for not making him go to the Doctor more often. I had tremendous guilt for not being able to remember CPR. In my state of shock, when I was waiting for the paramedics, I thought, "I'm supposed to do something for him, what is it? How do I do it? Later, I felt terrible that I had failed him.

I grew angry with friends who avoided me. Especially those that were so wrapped up in their lives that they barely acknowledged my loss. I was angry with the doctors when the autopsy came back and it said he wasn't intubated properly in the emergency room. Would it have made a difference if he had been?

Most of all, I was angry with God. He could have healed him and he didn't! The verse in Isaiah 54, that God would be my husband, wasn't initially comforting. I wanted MY husband. I wanted Milt.

It was a bit different when Robert died. I accepted the fact he was dead more quickly, but my depression lasted longer due to the fact that extra circumstances were involved. The hardest one was that my youngest son had come home to die. His faith convictions prevented him from taking the insulin that his diabetic body needed. That whole scenario kept me from grieving the loss of Robert until later. Multiple reasons to grieve compounded the grief work and made it harder. (Thankfully, my son didn't die, but he was debilitated for a long time even after he went back on insulin.)

After Milt died, I noticed that I was more fearful than I had been. If this could happen to my beloved, what else could happen to me? What else might be taken from me? Would my children die next? My sister? Or me? I had never locked the door before my husband's death, but now I dead-bolted the door and distributed keys to my four grown children.

On the other hand, I was ready to take more risks because death didn't seem like such a bad thing, it was almost welcome—but, then, that was from the depression I felt.

Stage 3: Bargaining

This was how I bargained with God, (as if I could make Him change His mind.) "If I had done—this or that—he might have lived." "If I promise to — maybe Milt can come back."

Over and over I would let my imagination run riot. I'd imagine ways I could have prevented my husband's death. No one would believe the creative things I came up with. Of course, it did little good—he was still dead.

I had a lot of nighttime dreams in this stage, too, dreams that actually helped me because they provided some closure. I would see Milt come running into the house, wearing a nice suit, carrying his Bible. He would give me a quick kiss and say that he'd be back soon. He never could stay for long. One time, he kissed me on the lips and I felt it. When I awoke, I was lying there with my finger pressed against my lips. I was sad when I awoke, but still the dreams made me feel close to him.

Stage 4: Depression

I have always been a happy person. My grief came over me with heavy depression, nothing like I'd ever felt before. When I felt sad in the past, the feeling would last one day or for a part of a day. Often reading some scripture and hearing an inspiring song would help. I would pray and give the pain, hurt, or sadness to God and the feeling would lift.

This cloud of blackness didn't leave me when I tried my usual coping methods. Conversely, if I was happy for just a moment, I felt guilty. But the reality was hitting me. He will never come back through that door again; we'd never see the sunset together, lie in each other's arms, laugh and cry together, or pray holding hands.

Later, I found out that once you got to the depression stage, if you grieved well, it could mean that healing was on the way. That would have given me hope. But I wonder if I would have believed it.

Stage 5: Acceptance

The wound is finally beginning to heal. I was beginning to have longer periods of being happy. I didn't cry every time I thought of my loved one. In this stage, I began to enjoy my memories.

I felt ready to try new things again. My heart didn't hurt as much as it had. I felt I could try a new activity or a new hobby. I was willing to do things I'd never done before. There still were times of sadness and loneliness. I found that life seemed more precious and so were my relationships. Things were not taken for granted as they might have been before. I began to feel proud of myself for moving on.

If we could do this grieving in order, it would be easier. Unfortunately, often we go two steps forward and one back in this grief journey. I would think, "oh good, now I'm through that stage" but then similar trials would repeat themselves. Around and around the mountain of grief and pain I would go. I came to realize that the closer you were in relationship to your beloved, the more complex, the harder, would be the process of healing. When I realized this, I became more patient with myself. I became gentler with my own expectations and took things one day at a time.

I can imagine you might be saying, "This is too hard. I want my pain healed right now." Unfortunately, it will have to run its course. The thing you must understand is that "God will always bring something

good out of this terrible thing when you love Him."
(Romans 8:28 paraphrased).

It is too high a price, we think. But as long as we
must experience it, it is helpful to know that God's
redemptive light is going to shine on you. And, yes,
"good" is coming.

Workbook-Chapter Two

Please be honest as you do these exercises. God knows the doubts and fears and other emotions that are in your mind and heart. His love is constant no matter what. Even if you have negative thoughts, put them down. Admitting them brings them into the light and into healing.

❖ *Psalm 89:48-NIV*
What man can live and not see death, or save himself from the power of the grave?

Why are we shocked by death? We are in denial in this society. We avoid thinking of death and try to hold it off with vitamins and special workouts and eating right. How can we be more aware of death's reality or is it better to deal with it when it comes?

❖ Psalm 69:3 — NIV
I am worn out calling for help: my throat is parched: my eyes fail, looking for my God.

It is healthy to grieve. But there must be times of balance. It might help to be with young children because they are so free and full of life. They also give good hugs. Some enjoy animals, one's own pets, or find a trip to the Zoo is helpful.

It is good to cry and then to refrain from crying. My therapist said, "Allow yourself a half hour to cry and then do something else."

What lifts your spirits?

❖ *Psalm 90:12-NIV*
So teach us to number our days aright, that we may gain a heart of wisdom.

What gives your life meaning now?

_____

❖ Psalm 90:15-NIV
Make us glad according to the days you have afflicted us, and the years wherein we have seen evil.

What is the hope that you have now?

_____

❖ Psalm 16:11—NIV
You have made known to me the path of life: you will fill me with joy in your presence, with eternal pleasures at your right hand.

Ask God to show you your unique path and restore you to the joy in His presence.

❖ Psalm 5:12—NIV
For surely O Lord, you will bless the righteous; you surround him with your favor as with a shield.

Pray this Psalm putting your name in where it says "righteous." Put "her" if you are a woman, "him" if you are a man. Remember, we are *righteous* because of Jesus, so don't be afraid to really own these words of promise.

Spend time in prayer with others. Let God know your needs, pain and troubles. Hold up the others during the week. It is so helpful to change your focus for a while and see the hearts of others. You are not alone.

Chapter Three

What if . . .

The grief support group saved me from despair. I desperately needed others who could relate to my experiences. There was a great need to make sense of what had happened. I asked "What if?" What if Milt had gone to the doctor on Monday when he told me he felt anxiety? That might have been a signal from his heart that he was in trouble.

My second husband Robert questioned, "What if we hadn't lived near the river (that some thought caused cancer.")

Wanting to help others, Robert and I formed a support group for people who were grieving. We allowed the members to have a safe place to share their questions and experiences. (After Robert died, I continued leading the group.)

We invited anyone from our congregation to join us who were suffering from loss of any kind. Those who attended consistently were the ones who had lost a spouse. Any form of grief is significant, but we noted that the death of a life partner seemed to be the most intense.

I had never experienced the loss of a child, another traumatic event that is very painful. Multiple crisis's plagued me during the time of my youngest son's near-death episode right after Robert's death. Then devastating financial problems and a betrayal of a friend was more than I could bear alone. How I appreciated the group I'd formed, as the members comforted me in one of the darkest times in my life.

We were never meant to walk alone. God gave Eve to Adam; Jesus sent His disciples out two-by-two. The New Testament Scriptures exhort us to not forsake gathering together in fellowship. I believe this was critical to my ability to grieve well. If you haven't yet found caring prayer partners, look for them. God will show you who they are.

The Nagging "If Onlys"

Oh, the nagging whispers of "If only" just wouldn't leave me alone. I couldn't seem to stop trying to make sense of my husbands' deaths. I still flirt with that "If only" phrase, upon seeing one of my grandchildren say something funny or smart, like Gabriel piping up with, "I've learned a lot in my seven years." Then I wish that Milt could have seen at least one of our eight grandchildren.

People often say something like this to me, "Well, of course, he sees them from heaven." I've never read that in the Bible, though I hope it is true. When my first beautiful granddaughter was born, I imagined that God let Milt hold her before she came to earth. Someone had sent me a picture of him holding a baby girl just before he baptized her. It was easy to imagine her as our little Alyssa. I hold that picture in my heart just as I do a prayer.

My friend Dan knows about "if only." He kissed his wife goodbye in their cozy farm kitchen. She was on her way back to work and in an instant both Dan and his wife's lives changed. That December day, there was glare ice on the road. Another car was coming toward her. It doesn't matter whose fault it was, they hit head-on. The other person lived, but she died.

If only she hadn't driven that day . . . *if only* they had salted the road. . . *if only* she would have survived the crash. If only.

Another friend, Bob, who also adored his wife, understood this state of mind. She was diagnosed with Alzheimer's in her fifties. He watched her beauty being ravaged, her personality change until she was childlike. Still, he thought her beautiful in that innocent state and, for years, he lovingly cared for her. When she died, he was angry with God. "If only." But like me, he came to peace with his loss. His heart is still totally hers and God's. He is one of the most loving people I know, using his time to help many others in need.

What if Robert, my second husband, could have realized his sedentary life might lead to his death? Always a big man, he never had time to exercise due to his long daily commute. Even a short walk made him breathless. I wondered "what if" a change in his eating habits could have kept him alive.

Saying "if only" and "what if" is a common way of working through one's questions. Of course, this is only a coping measure. Nothing can be changed and one needs to finally let the questions go in order to have peace.

When I thought about the "If onlys," I became distracted from living in the now. I lived in a mind-set that was lost in grief. I found that when I was experiencing pain and loss, I became easily upset over things that wouldn't ordinarily bother me.

Or I would be absentminded. I would sometimes be driving in my car not remembering where I was going. That can happen when you have too many things on your mind, at any time in your life, but it also happens to those experiencing grief. Sometimes, I felt like I was losing my mind.

Another "If only" I experienced was about money. If, before Milt's death, I had known how to handle our finances, my life in survival mode would have been easier. Milt had tried to sit down with me periodically to explain things, but I listened with half an ear. What if I had listened to my spouse when he talked about our finances? I would have saved myself a ton of worry. Turns out my income after Milt was more than sufficient. I finally learned how to efficiently take care of my finances several years after he died. I wish I had known all along. In this case, knowledge truly was power.

Some men can't cook or sew on a button. With more women working, this is changing, but many still don't know how to take care of themselves or their homes.

For example, I sometimes gave homemade dinners to my father-in-law after his wife (my mother-in-law) died. He lived close by and had dinner with us most evenings, but occasionally we were away at dinnertime, and then I would deliver his meal. One day when I opened his freezer to put in my latest offering, I noticed that none of the packaged dinners had been used. When I asked about this, he sheepishly replied that he didn't know how to turn on the oven!

It can be terribly disheartening for a surviving husband to look inside the fridge and find veggies wearing "fur caps" and cheese sporting blue polka dots.

I tell all my happily married friends to think about the "what ifs." Get to know your finances, learn how to put the furnace filter in, or whatever your husband or wife does that you know little about. This is plain common sense, but often my friends are in denial.

What if I would have paid more attention to other roles or jobs that I took for granted? My husband made sure the car had its oil changes and other car maintenance. I knew nothing about those things. I came from a generation that had distinct roles.

The mind of the grieving person can't take in the immensity of the loss all at once. At any rate, the "if onlys" and "what ifs" will eventually subside, and one is left with reality. Remember, the "what ifs" are a means to an end. They are another task or phase of the grief process. They help us to move through this hard time. Don't give up hope; it WILL get better.

Workbook — Chapter 3

Martha said, "If only you had been here, then Lazarus would not have died."

Oh, Martha, how I understand you! I would have said the same thing.

Jesus was told that his friend Lazarus was dying. He tarried several days and then went. Lazarus' sisters, Martha and Mary, couldn't understand why he didn't come and heal him. Jesus had His reasons, as explained in the text. Chapter 11 of John's gospel tells us it was "for God's glory."

We, as mourners, ask the same question. (If only You had been here.) Jesus, where were you? In our situation, Jesus WAS there. We may not have seen Him, but the hands of our Savior were touching our situation.

He did not condone violence.

He wept along with us as we saw our loved one ravaged by disease.

He had pity when he saw us stumbling and bumbling in grief and shock calling out, "Oh God, where are you?" He whispered "Here I am my child," but perhaps we couldn't hear.

❖ Psalm 103:13-14-NIV
As a father has compassion on his children, so the Lord has compassion on those who fear* Him; for He knows how we are formed, He remembers they we are dust.

*Fear in this sense means, "honor and believe in.

To honor and believe in your earthly father, wouldn't you need to trust in the goodness in His heart? That's what we can do with our Heavenly Father.

Have you seen any touch of God in your "What ifs"? Do you have any thoughts that start with "at least?"

Please list any below; for example: At least, she knew you…or

At least, we had many happy times lately.

_____

_____

_____

❖ Is. 40:11-NIV-

He tends His flock like a shepherd, He gathers the lambs in His arms, and carries them close to His heart.

Do you sense God holding you in His arms against His breast? How does it comfort you? Does he say anything to you? If you don't sense this, why not, do you think? Spend some time picturing yourself there.

If you wish, write your thoughts here.

_____

_____

_____

❖ Luke 7:11a-13 — NIV-

Jesus went to a town called Nain. He and the group that was traveling with Him saw a bier being carried out, and upon it was the corpse of a young man. He was the only son of his mother, and she was a widow. When the Lord saw her, His heart went out to her and He said, "Don't cry."

Jesus had compassion on people and it is shown over and over how He met all their needs. He said, "I am the Resurrection and the Life." and "… He who believes in Me will live, even though he dies …"

We have the glorious hope of heaven and will reunite with our loved ones.

Jesus raised the son of the widow of Nain so that she would not only have her son back, but that son would take care of her. There were no pension plans or insurance policies in those days. Widows with no family, could end up starving unless someone took pity on them.

Jesus' compassion was his strongest characteristic. Can you remember a time or times when you felt His compassion in an experience or an answered prayer? Please record this below.

_____

_____

_____

We wonder why our loved one had to die when we hear of someone else's miraculous recovery. Pray your questions. Don't be afraid. His answers might not come in ways that you thought they would, but sense His love for you even in His silence.

Hold these truths from the Scriptures in your heart: *Your ways are not mine. I will trust in you.*

If you sense God sharing a word or a feeling of peace, note it here.

_____

_____

_____

It is okay to tell God that you can't hear Him. Recording artist Sara Groves sings a song to the Lord that is something like this: "Right now I can't hear so well, and I was wondering if you could speak up." She later says she is willing to wait for His answer. Waiting is one of our *tasks*.

Chapter Four

Burying Grief or Walking Through It

I have never been one to bury my feelings. I need to talk about my troubles, but my dearest friends can't always listen to my pain. So I have learned to talk first to God. My emotions spill out quite well into my journals.

"If I die before I wake, throw my journal in the lake!" I don't want to offend anyone after I'm gone; maybe I better put these instructions in my will.

Friends and family, though they try, can't always understand what you're going through. As a grief counselor, I know many grieving ones who have tried stuffing away their pain. A mother whose baby died in her womb was told that she had other children and to "get over it." Similarly, a wife whose husband was dead only a few months, was told to "move on." It is okay to let grief take its time. The people mentioned were hurt by the above comments and tried to bury their feelings only to prolong the agony.

Whatever grief you bury will reappear later in another form.

Often men and sometimes women, bury themselves in their jobs so that they can't, or won't, feel their pain. The grief will still be there to be dealt with later.

My second husband Robert did this. When his first wife died, he offered to work longer hours, so he wouldn't have to spend so much time alone. These are his words from one of the grief seminars we gave:

"I would come home from work in the evenings to an empty house. I was trying so hard for life to be normal. I would read the paper or watch TV as always. The only difference was that I would talk to Darlene about things, and then realize she wasn't there. The result was always that I would lie down and hope that I wouldn't have to get up again. I didn't want to *feel* and that is a kind of death.

I found myself working 12 to 14 hour days and bringing work home so I could bury myself and keep my mind occupied. My time became one mass of fruitless endeavors, making busy work rather than accomplishing meaningful projects.

My wife's relatives lived in my town and they pretty much ignored me. They had their own pain. Some wouldn't even speak to me on the street. I was truly alone."

Another burying method is to numb the pain. Partaking in addictive substances, drugs, or alcohol, is a coping method for some. These things cannot fill the void caused by loss. Food and drink can be misused, either by eating or drinking too much or, conversely, by "forgetting to eat." Grieving pain just hurts so badly people try to find relief by using forms of painkillers.

Sadly, this is no way to live. God wants us to live abundant, meaningful lives—He never intended us to barely exist, He wants us alive and well.

Another "coping" method is isolation. This comes from depression, which is a normal part of losing a spouse or dear one. But hiding away, as one friend of mine did, and not answering the door or phone, makes suicide a greater possibility. She admitted later she was thinking of taking her life. One day she told me that my telephone messages I'd left on her answering machine caused her to choose life. That taught me how much good just a simple thing could do.

Everyone seems so busy, so it's rare when some one really listens to you. We learn that after awhile, some folks don't want you to talk about your feelings of grief anymore. They want you to be "fixed."

They seem uncomfortable that there is still anguish. They may act nervous or change the subject. So even if you want to talk, you are instinctively aware that you can't share how you really feel with certain people. You start to say "Fine," when you are asked how you are even when you don't feel that way.

After a time, we who grieve are tired of talking about our losses too. We desperately want to move on and yet we still hurt so much. It's a hard place to be.

Your Pathway to Healing

It helps to spend time with other mourners, but we cannot judge their experiences. We should not compare ourselves to anyone else. Each person's marriage relationship, or loss, was uniquely different. And no personality is the same.

Each person must find his or her own way to grieve well. There are as many ways as there are people. I decided to look at my experiences differently. I looked at grief as a positive pathway to healing, not as something negative. This was an approach I could live with. I wanted to know I was on *that* path.

Here are some of the negative things that I began to think of as being positive. First, I found others who needed to talk as much as I did. No more did I feel badly for wanting to talk about my pain.

It is important to get your feelings out in some way. You can tell God in writing and prayer, or tell friends or coun-selors. Keeping it all inside can be toxic. Healing can come through the companionship of those who have listening ears, if only people knew the healing power of listening. What a wonderful gift to give someone.

Find ways to express your pain in words. Stay with the pain and feel the hurt. Write it out! Yell it out! I tried that when in the car where no one else could hear. Just don't have your windows open.

Start thinking of time as a friend, not an enemy. Use your time thoughtfully. Treat yourself as an injured patient, realizing that this is your time of recovery. Like physical therapy to injured limbs, try taking steps that will help you improve. Things must change and cannot go back to the way they were. Realizing this is a major part of recovery.

It's important to get enough rest. Grief takes a tremendous amount of energy. I had to learn to say no to things at times when I needed to re-energize. These are common sense things, but often we need to give ourselves permission to simply take care of ourselves.

For example, may need to tell people if you are not ready to have company. Once a well-meaning friend wanted to come to stay with me in the very early stages of grief. Maybe a couple of days would have been fine, but I told her she could stay longer and it turned out to be too long. It was nice to have someone else in the house, but I didn't feel free to cry while she was here. I remember driving home from taking her to the airport. I let it rip, weeping all the way home. For me daily periods of sobbing were necessary to pour out my feelings. I didn't think she would understand that, so I had been holding back. Of course, maybe she would have understood if I had explained it. I wish I had tried.

I found a few things that were positive helps while in this stage of early recovery. I listened to beautiful music and enjoyed art – these things can be healing anytime. Little pursuits that free us momentarily from the sadness also help. Exercise, and participating in sports are excellent for body, mind, and soul. We need fresh air and sunshine. Taking a vacation with friends is very healing. Always we take our grief with us, but new surroundings can help. For me, getting away was excellent, although I missed my spouse and wished he were with me. Though I had to return home to an empty house, I would plan something fun in order to lessen the lonely feeling.

Some have found hobbies, cooking, crafting, writing, building something, doing chores that show results, such as redecorating are helpful. Just don't sit in your home day after day. Get out and engage in life.

The first year after my husband died, I planted a garden in his honor. I normally did not garden, but Milt had always loved to tend the soil. He took pride in the fresh vegetables and luscious fruit. So I gardened in his honor. I felt so close to him in this simple way. There is something healing about working the soil, the freshness of outdoors, and seeing things grow. Then I never gardened again, except my flowers in pots. I enjoyed others gardens instead.

One woman I know created beautiful silk flower arrangements to work out her grief. A man used his talents by making toys for poor children.

These things do not take away the pain, but they help to focus on something else besides your grief and yourself. Do not "bury" yourself in the task, but notice what helps you find meaning in your everyday life. Enjoy small simple pleasures. A friend's phone call, or a hot cup of cocoa. A spider's web covered with dewdrops, or the beauty of the first leaves in Spring.

Each person moves through grief at his or her own pace. Even though I wanted to plow through it to get to the other side, I had to go slower than I wanted. One of the gifts in grief is the deepening in compassion for others that comes. I'm more aware of the brevity of life and want to live each moment more fully. Walking through grief is not pleasant, but a necessary path. I assure you, God will be walking by your side all the way.

What About Anger at God?

There was a period of months where I was extremely angry with God. I couldn't feel God's presence. The suddenness of Milt's death and the "unfairness" of it angered me and drove me away from God. I made a decision that turned out to be a good one. I kept talking to the Lord, even though I was angry with Him. I told Him exactly how I felt. This was a helpful thing for me, because I got it out in the open.

Some may think, who is she that she dares to question God? But if it was in my mind, God knew what I was thinking anyway. So I continued to pray and be honest with how angry I felt. Gradually I noticed a shift in my talks with Him. I read the Psalms and found every emotion in there. This gave me permission to tell God my true feelings because I could so easily relate to many of them. I continued to read them and other Scriptures daily. I prayed and asked for help in spite of my anger. It seemed as if God had moved away from me, but I knew in my spirit that He was within reach. I began to ask for a closer walk with Him and tell Him that I needed His forgiveness for my angry attitude.

A surprising event came about. I was asked to teach a retreat in the spring, a year and a half after Milt's death. Oh, perhaps you can imagine how I felt. I still thought I had nothing to say. The person who asked me to lead it assured me, saying, "Nancy, I know you're to be the speaker for this retreat."

Since I had kept my heart open to God, I told her I would try. I sat down in a quiet place to prepare a message. As I wrote, something like healing oil soothed my spirit, and the words I prepared became my love letter to God! That was a big breakthrough for me! Like Job, I was humbled, but very grateful that God is so faithful and forgiving. I wrote down all God gave me. As I drove home from that retreat with the big beautiful sun above, my heart was singing again. There still was grief work ahead of me, but I had entered a new period in my life.

I had wanted to know that the pain of my suffering would count for something. Many at the retreat told me that they were blessed by the sharing. Meaning was coming back into my life once more, and God was definitely right by my side.

Workbook–Chapter Four

I was excited again about God's promises and His love. I saw that I had learned valuable lessons in the "fire" of my trials. Yes, I felt the price for these lessons was too high, but the trial was there and the choice to learn or not was mine.

The possibility of drying up and shriveling was there too. I knew that if I didn't grow, I might never again touch anyone for Jesus. I saw that there was a lesson of Jesus in the tomb; it didn't hold Him back and it shouldn't stop me either.

❖ Job 13:15-NIV
Though He slay me, yet will I hope in Him.

Job's declaration became mine. I wanted all of Jesus' resurrection power.

The Lord says in

❖ Joshua 1:9—NIV
Be strong and courageous. Do not be terrified; do not be discouraged for the Lord is with you wherever you go.

When you meditate (think deeply) on these words, write down the promises that the Lord makes to you.

❖ Proverbs 3:5-NIV _____
_____
_____
_____

Trust the Lord with all your heart and lean not on your own understanding. In all your ways, acknowledge Him and He will make your paths straight.

Stay with this Scripture in your meditation and let in sink into your innermost being. When you feel ready, answer these questions:

1-How do I show God I trust Him?

_____

_____

_____

2-How do I acknowledge Him in ALL my ways?

_____

_____

_____

3-Write down ways in which He has already directed your path.

_____

_____

_____

The following are more promises of Your God. Write anything you want to tell him after meditating (thinking deeply) about them. When we reflect on scripture, we savor each word slowly until we come to one where we sense we should rest. Even if you reflect on part of a verse, it will be beneficial. You can come back to these later. Do not try to do them all at once.

❖ John 14:18-KJV
I will not leave you comfortless; I will come to you.

_____

_____

_____

❖ Ephesians 1:18-19-KJV

The eyes of your understanding being enlightened that you may know what is the hope of His calling, and the riches of the glory of inheritance in the saints, and what is the exceeding greatness of His power to we who believe, according to the working of His mighty power.

_____

_____

_____

❖ Psalm 145:14-NKJV

The Lord upholds all those who fall, and raises all who are bowed down.

_____

_____

_____

❖ John 10:27-28-KJV

My sheep hear my voice and I know them; they follow me. And I will give to them eternal life and they shall never perish, neither shall any man pluck them out of my hand.

_____

_____

_____

Chapter Five

Crazy Anniversaries

There is a song my mother used to sing about the way you wear your hat, the way you sang (not very well), and how no one can take those memories of you away from me.

Memories are made of smiles and tears. Reliving experiences with your loved one are what my friend Liz named "crazy anniversaries" for me. We expect to remember them on special anniversary days. It could be their birthday or our own, a holiday like Christmas, or our "wedding anniversary, the anniversary of their death—those kind of normal anniversaries. What's surprising is the pain that pierces our hearts on the crazy anniversaries.

Let me explain. I see a tool or a tie that he loved and that makes me sad. It may be that a small town event, like "the running of the smelt" will trigger a memory of his passion for fishing. I'll pass a park bench where we once used to sit. I'd smell a yellow rose and remember the one he gave me as a surprise once. We call these instances "crazy anniversaries." They can cause tears and pain and they come when you least expect them.

Of course, the memories might be wonderful in themselves, but it is the stinging reminder that your beloved one is gone and you can't even see or hug the person you miss so very much.

There is a song with lyrics that go something like this: "I'd walk a million miles to see one of your smiles." When a person is gone from us, the ache is just so painful. Any little memory can trigger immense sorrow.

We are bound to remember a loved one in surprising ways. This is normal. In our group, we were willing to make special plans, a time of fun, with someone who was having an expected anniversary. In this way, we could help take the edge off the difficult day. But you just never know when a "crazy anniversary" will pop up.

Whenever they hit me, I found crying a little and journaling about it helped. Or I'd tell a friend about it.

I tried to turn the memory's hurt into gratefulness. These moments will happen and they can be celebrated as well as grieved. Sometimes, I'll say something like, "I had a beloved one who will always love me. We had this special time together or memory. Because he was so dear to me is why this bothers me. Thank you God, for this moment that I cherish in my heart, even if it hurts."

Memories that Heal

Another part of this loss business, is the small things that we don't expect to grieve. This week I was grieving the loss of my car, which was hit by a drunk driver as we drove through downtown Kansas City. When the other driver came up to our car afterwards to ask if we were all right, we noticed that his eyes were red-rimmed and his breath smelled of alcohol. He wouldn't give us his insurance information, saying he would give it to the police. Then he said he would pull up in the next block, but, instead, he drove away.

The whole episode brought back memories of a much worse accident in 1977. Milt and our children were on our way to my parents' house in Indiana. Milt was driving and may have fallen asleep. Suddenly, we went off the road, rolled into the median strip and hit a culvert that caused us to fly through the air. We landed very hard; my back felt the hard jolt. I will never forget the crunching sound of rippling glass breaking as the windshield disintegrated before our eyes. The end result for me was a crushed vertebra that eventually healed well. The physical healing process took a year and, at that time, I wondered if I would ever have energy again.

The breaking of the window during the second accident triggered the memory of the past one. I felt overwhelming sorrow that resulted from overreacting to the present accident. When I recalled how serious the past one was, the present one seemed like a small thing. But acknowledging the first accident helped me release the lost and shaken-up feeling.

I had thought that the accident in 1977 had been healed and forgotten. It is amazing how we recall old memories when other things jiggle our remembering. Sometimes this sadness is caused by not completing the grieving in the earlier incident. Often these little losses can surprise you with their intensity.

Recognizing these things can help to alleviate our concern and tell us why we feel so "down." In my case, when I compared the two incidents, I had lots of things to thank the Lord for. No one was hurt. The car was drivable. We could return to the Twin Cities where we lived. Insurance would cover the expenses, including a rental car for me to drive. Truly, there were many things for which I could be grateful — both times.

I've learned that, when I am grieving something, I need to examine it a bit closer. I recognize it, come to better understand it, and then let it go. This works better than saying "That is nothing, just forget about it." I feel free and healthy when I work things through.

You may have experienced something as a child that will affect the way you look at things now. Often younger children are not allowed to grieve the loss their loved ones. Or we fail to discuss their feelings with them. They easily can accept the idea that their grandmother, for example, has gone away to heaven and is with Jesus, so we may think they don't suffer any sorrow. However, they may need to talk about this a lot more than we realize.

In the past, death used to be hush-hush with children in most homes and, perhaps, it is still prevalent today. In fact, if your family was like that, you may have recurring issues that stem from not being able to discuss openly whatever bad things, or deaths, happened in your family. By taking these things to God in prayer, and by allowing His comfort to come, and forgiving the inability of family members to talk about your old hurts, God will heal those old sorrows and burdens you have carried for so long. Often, we don't realize how these things have affected us and still do.

My parents often mentioned my elder brother's birthday each January. Because of a serious birth defect, he only lived for three days. As a child growing up, I often wished that I could have had an older brother to look up to and protect me. I wondered what my life would have been like if he hadn't died. Because my parents remembered his birthday, I knew they still loved him. Even in my childlike mind, I knew that if I had died at birth, they would have still remembered and loved me too. This positive experience meant a lot to me. His life was meaningful to me even though I never saw him.

My granddaughter Alyssa loved Papa (Robert), as she called him. She was only four when he died, but they had shared a close relationship. When her friend Taylor's grandfather came to visit, it triggered her grief. She wailed, "I want my Papa! It's not fair." Her reaction was a healthy one and we acknowledged how she felt.

I experience joy and pain when I see something of my husband Milt in the grandchildren. I am sad that he never got to see or hold even one of them. He loved children and would have been a wonderful grandpa. I share things about him with the kids, but it's not the same. So when the little memories appear, I experience one of my crazy anniversaries. I shed a few tears; I hold the memory close for a bit and savor the moment of love. The pain is less than it used to be. And surprise memories are sometimes welcomed now. I have learned to thank God for my crazy anniversaries because they remind me that I had the chance to love and be loved.

Workbook—Chapter Five

❖ Psalm 143:1-NIV-
O Lord, hear my prayer, listen to my cry for mercy; in your faithfulness and righteousness come to my relief.

In this very emotional psalm of David, his anguish speaks to us. Two things stand out to me; cry for mercy and come to my relief. Our Lord is faithful and righteous and because of that He WILL come to my relief.

How has He come to your relief this week?

_____

_____

_____

Have you noticed sad moments that came out of the blue? What were they and what did they trigger?

_____

_____

_____

Often we get so caught up in grief, we don't see the sparkles. My special little grandson of three was riding with his Aunt and me. My sister was complaining about the rain that had accompanied her long drive to my house. Since it was night, Gabriel's little voice came from his seat in the darkness behind us.

"Look, Gram and Auntie, see the sparkles!" The light from the streetlight had touched the drops on the windshield making them beautiful in the eyes of my grandson. What a lesson he taught us that day! Ordinary raindrops can be beautiful when the light shines through them.

List the sparkles The Lord has put in your life in the last week. Include little things that most people don't see. Notice a dewdrop on a spider web, a kitten's purr and softness, a lovely sunset.

Sometimes tears are the sparkles. We think of tears as something bad. They are evidence of a caring heart. No one can take that away from us.

Can you think of other crazy anniversaries? What are some of yours you've experienced?

_____

_____

_____

What can you learn about yourself from them?

_____

_____

_____

Does sharing this help you? How?

_____

_____

_____

God says He will not forget us. He has written us or engraved us upon His hand.

_____

_____

_____

❖ Psalm 139: NKJ
And in your book they were written, the days fashioned for me, when as yet there were none of them.

How does it feel to know God will never forget you; in fact, he keeps track of every single day?

❖ Malachi 3:16,17-KJV

They that feared the Lord spoke often one to another.
And the Lord hearkened and heard it, and a book of
remembrance was written before him for them that
feared the Lord and thought on his name. They shall
be mine, said the Lord of hosts in that day when I make
up my jewels; and I will spare them, as a man spares
his own son that serves him.

Wow! You are His and you are a jewel! You are in his
book of remembrance. We thank you, Lord! Write down
the things in this passage that bless you most.

Chapter Six

Widowhood—the Club You Didn't Want to Join

"The Merry Widow" is a fictional idea. I obviously wasn't merry. I certainly didn't expect widowhood to come until my 90s. Both Milt and I were in excellent health. Certainly, we'd enjoy a long time together. I had no idea how hard it would be to live without my best friend and lover. When I heard people refer to me as a "widow" in the early days after his death, I couldn't stand it. It shocked me.

I went to the Social Security office several weeks after my husband's death. My friend, who came with me, and I heard our feet echo down the huge, marble halls of the courthouse. The sound was cold, and impersonal. After a lengthy time in the waiting room, my name was called. The interviewer began with a series of questions, one of which unnerved me.

"When did the marriage end?" he asked in a disinterested voice. I wanted to scream that it hadn't ended, because that sounded like divorce. *I was still married to Milt, wasn't I?*

I hated the question, but with a dull and dragging voice I told him the date of my beloved's death. Just being in the courthouse office was painful and the man was doing his job, but I resented him.

It got worse. After doing some calculations on his computer, the administrator told me I would be getting zilch, nada, nothing, because Milt was one quarter shy of the quota for receiving Social Security payments. Now I heard this at a time when I didn't know anything of my financial situation. My bank account was nearly empty from funeral costs, flying one of my sons home from Europe, and other expenses.

Then the man had the nerve to say, "I'm sure glad I never had *the Call*," referring to Milt's pastoral status. Since I was proud of my husband and his spiritual calling, that hurt more than anything. Certainly, this man was ridiculously insensitive.

The friend who accompanied me was sympathetic when I told her about the interview. I cried all the way home. I later called the office and complained about the man's behavior, but could not remember his name. I experienced griever's confusion and inability to respond at the time. It felt like my mind was spinning out of control.

That was the first of many experiences that made me realize I was a member of a club that I hadn't wanted to join. Many people said things to me that were nice or caring. Even those that said things that hurt, certainly meant well. Perhaps they didn't know what to say.

Once a friend of my sister's unthinkingly blurted out, "Just think of all the years you have to be a widow." *Thanks a lot*, I thought. I hadn't begun thinking in terms of years yet. I wondered how in the world was I was going to get through the next few days, the next month; how would I live *at all* without my husband?

When I talked to others in the same "club" I heard stories of some hurtful things people had said to them. I remembered the past years when I didn't know what to say to a new widow. Had I said things that were offensive? I hoped not. I realized then that people are trying, but don't always think through what they say.

Even harder than the well-meaning hurtful things people said to me were the flippant words of advice people gave — like "you should be over it by now." Then there were those who avoided me because they were at a loss for words and didn't want to face me.

I didn't expect life to turn into such a mess. I had imagined I would be able to handle such a loss fairly well, if it came along. I felt good about myself. As husband and wife, we worked at being interdependent, not dependant. I am an extrovert but I also love solitude and silence. I led a balanced, healthy life. As far as losing a life partner, the part I hadn't thought about was the "forever" aspect, or another way of putting it, the "never again" part.

When Milt was alive, I would return from a conference or retreat, and he would ask me about my time away, and I would do the same when he went away. We loved sharing our experiences. He once wrote a poem about me being gone entitled "Nancy is not here." It made me so aware of his deep love and that, while I was away, he missed me.

Mornings were hard. Before Milt died, he would often get up before me to pray, but he always returned to our bedroom to kiss me. We would pray together and exercise before one of us had to leave for the day. Now there was a gaping hole in my morning routine that would never be filled with Milt again.

And evenings were worse, aching and wishing for him to come home. It just would not, could not, be. One night, needing a warm body beside me, I put my huge brown teddy bear in bed with me on Milt's side of the bed. At dawn, I sleepily looked over there and saw the outline of a huge bear's nose. I nearly screamed until I realized, oh yes, my teddy bear.

How I hated the widow's "club." I was angry when a friend told me that she thought that my ministry would be helping other people who lost spouses. I was still in denial, not wanting to believe her words. I didn't want the job. I ended up doing just what she said, but, at the time, I wasn't ready to receive her prophetic words.

When I met my second husband, life seemed to open up again. We vowed that together we would help others as we had been helped. Four short years later, Robert died. I did not want to be angry with God again. It was hard to go through this so soon. I had believed that my marriage to Robert was God's will for me. It was, but right after he died, I questioned the logic of God's plan. And I was back in the dreaded club.

I kept asking God why He allowed me to go through such a difficult thing twice. Then I heard a tape by a missionary doctor named Helen who asked God the same type of question for a different reason. She had been helping Africans with various health problems. During a coup within the government, a rebel soldier raped her. "Why God, Why?" she cried.

God's answer to her was, "Can you trust me even if I never tell you why?"

I realized that God didn't have to tell me why. But when I least expected it, He did.

"I allowed this because I trust you," He seemed to say. This helped me, though I don't fully understand it. It is one of those "seeing through a glass darkly" things.

If someone shares, with a downcast look, "I just lost my husband, or wife," and you respond, "Me too," you are a member of the "club." There is an instantaneous bond formed. There is no special handshake for the special association but the password is "Me too."

People in this club understand the initial confusion of "Who am I now that my partner is gone?"

Also, there are club "dues" to pay. The dues are to pick up the jobs or chores he or she used to do. Family members go through their own adjustments.

Also, the "initiation" into this club is a time of confusion, not only for oneself, but also for family members. Some try to help too much, depending on their personalities, some want to ignore what's happening, and some run the other way.

My grown children missed their dad's corny jokes and teasing him about health foods he liked such, as wheat germ, and brewer's yeast. That was fun to remember. Occasionally, I'd glimpse their pain. Seeing their loss at times added to my sadness and uncertainty. We had bittersweet discussions. That was one kind of healing with my children and another with my grieving friends.

I found that during this early initiation into the club of mourners, I could lean heavily on my fellow members. I learned to trust the bond between myself and them. We supported and learned from each other. Often, we even found humor to share, and that is so important to healing. We could laugh together because we had cried together.

My favorite story of the grief support group is about a woman who admitted that she liked to wear her husband's old work shirt because it made her feel close to him. That precipitated another person who said that he'd seen an elderly man go to the drive-through at the bank wearing a hat that looked feminine and probably was his deceased wife's.

Another man spoke up and replied, "I'm just trying to picture myself in my wife's high heels." We all roared with laughter.

Some of my married friends helped me to feel more normal by including me in their activities. When I felt better, I wanted to do something for them. When some friends put on an addition to their house, I brought dinner. It gave me a chance to join them in the meal and provided something they needed. It felt good to help someone else and got me thinking about others instead of myself. I wanted to be *me* instead of "a widow."

At first, I could do little more than take care of the bare essentials of life. I was gentle with myself, but also learned to push myself a little.

Some people have found that helping to combat the disease that caused their loved one's death could be a way of dealing with grief and loneliness. Fundraising Cancer walks, Heart Research, Alzheimer's walks, runs for MS, and other opportunities are available.

When people offered to help me, I would take it. People want to help and I needed the support. 'Tough guys' often turn down help and make it harder on themselves and everyone else around them. We were made to be relational, to support one another and give encouragement. Don't try to be alone ranger.

I'll repeat the saying, "Shared burdens are halved, and shared joys are multiplied." I believe it so strongly. People's prayers and help got me through. I felt loved and encouraged by many.

Grieving was tough. I do not minimize it. Some days I really didn't think I *could* go on living. Other days I didn't *want to go on.* For all I cared, the "club" could exist without me. Some days, it is all one can do to show up for the day. But please, don't give up.

Workbook-Chapter Six

Here is a prayer I found. I think it is appropriate for the widowhood club.

Lord, may I settle it once and for always, I am dealing directly with you.

You need never apologize for any plan you ordain for me, since nothing but goodness can come from your hand. You are sufficient for every changing circumstance in my God-planned life. Amen.

❖ Psalm 56:8 KJV
YOU tell of my wanderings. YOU put my tears in a bottle: are they not in your book?

If you can, read the above prayer, and then rewrite it in your own words. Example: Dear Lord, You care about me so much that you know where I wander. My tears are so valuable that you store them away in a wineskin or bottle.

❖ Psalm 6:6-NIV
I am worn out with groaning; all night I flood my bed with weeping and drench my couch with tears.

Now, Words of Hope— Put your name in these verses.

❖ Psalm 116:7,8,9-NIV
Be at rest once more O my soul, for the Lord has been good to you. For you, O Lord have delivered my soul from death, my eyes from tears and my feet from stumbling that I may walk with the Lord in the land of the living.

_____

_____

_____

_____

Promise for the Future—
The Lord will wipe away your tears.

❖ Is. 25:8-NIV
He will swallow up death forever. The Sovereign Lord will wipe tears from all faces.

Chapter Seven

Wishing for What Might Have Been

When I was a little girl, my mother read fairy tale romances to me. I discovered after Milt and I were married, that living with a spouse means continually working together and working things out. Love alone didn't make it easy, but commitment and true dialogue helped. Milt and I were committed to each other for life. We made a conscious choice to always listen, even if we disagreed. We believed God brought us together, to love and cherish one another through whatever life would bring us. Respect was central to our relationship and made it easy to forbear each other's foibles. We weren't perfect, but we were in love for over three decades.

Hard times came and went, but the problems we dealt with were almost always from outside circumstances, not from within our relationship. Our commitment of loving God, love for one another, and trust never failed us; we were happy.

My biggest regret was that I did not get a chance to say goodbye to him. I didn't have time to hold him and tell him once more how much I loved him. After I called 911, I continued to pray for him. Once the paramedics got there I couldn't get near, I had to let them do their work. I wouldn't let any thoughts of death enter my mind. I refused to look at him. I wanted only victory in this scenario. Remembering the experience, I would relive the event and wonder how I could have done things differently. Eventually, I released my sorrow concerning this to Jesus.

Another one of my "wishes" concerned our grown children, how they missed their dad. I wished there was a way to talk to him about them. I also wished I could tell him about how the grandchildren had some of his characteristics. I could picture him playing with them and reveling in each one's unique personalities. But how could I tell him about these precious children? I decided to write letters to him and I asked God to be my messenger. This helped me to find some closure.

Seeing our parents cope with losing a spouse, Milt and I had thought a little about death — albeit at some future date. The only thing I remember about our conversation is that we had promised each other that we would try to "go on" when one of us died.

When I met Robert, I wondered how Milt would feel if he knew I was marrying again. I felt a little guilty about loving someone else.

Also, I still loved Milt. My emotions were in a whirl. After writing a letter telling Milt about my new life, loneliness without him, and God's provision of a wonderful man, I believed Milt would have wanted me to be happy and get married again. I assured Milt in "a letter" that I would always love him.

This new marriage was offering me a chance to love and be loved. Robert was a kind and loving man who was a good Christian. We were very well matched. I felt God was smiling down on this union, and that I had Milt's blessing too.

Some people in my grief group had regrets that were quite different than mine. They wished that they had talked more with their spouses, been honest and had not argued so much, or they wished they had been more on top of things and had taken preventive measures. A typical comment might be: "I wish my wife had taken better care of herself."

Regret factors were often involved smoking, excessive drinking, and overeating. Others were that one of the surviving spouses would wish they'd paid closer attention to symptoms and involved a doctor sooner. One friend thought the lump on her face would be healed and refused to have it checked by a doctor. It was too late to save her life by the time she discovered it was cancerous. Her death devastated her husband, children, and grandchildren.

Gary's wife, Sue, found a lump in her breast the year of her daughter's wedding. She decided to wait until after the event to go to the doctor and it proved to be a fatal mistake. He wished she had been more concerned about it. It is common to be angry with the deceased person when things could have been different had a better choice been made. Worse yet is to feel guilty about being angry.

The best way to get past regret is to forgive. If decisions were made that you couldn't control, realize this and forgive yourself and the loved one that erred. With God's help, forgive the one who couldn't control an addiction, forgive the one who was in denial about a fatal condition, and forgive the one who could have avoided death in some way. If you cannot forgive because you simply are unable to, ask God to help you. All you need to do is be willing to forgive. Often, forgiveness is a process. I have heard a counselor say, "You must forgive NOW." Forcing someone to forgive never works. Ask God to help you see things through His eyes— with His compassion, wisdom, and understanding. Be open to what He will show you. Sometimes it takes awhile. Our Lord knows the timing of these things.

This is how I have learned to pray in these kinds of situations. "Lord Jesus, I put your cross between this person and me." The cross is the symbol of Christ's victory for me. All that is wrong in my life and yours can be healed and forgiven. I am set free in the shadow of the cross. The feelings of forgiveness will come in time as I bask in the light of God's True Love. This is a prayer to "soak" in.

The "Saint" Issue

My friend Polly had a very difficult husband. She didn't complain much, but I knew he was demanding by the way he talked to her sometimes. He didn't understand the fervor she showed for the Lord. When he died, she talked about him unrealistically as if he had been the most wonderful husband ever.

After Milt's death, he became, in my mind, the most perfect man who had ever lived. He was a man of such Godly character; it was easy to put him on a pedestal. As a church pastor, he was highly respected by the congregation and his peers. During and after the funeral, many people told me of wonderful things he had done for them. Some marveled that he had made house calls, which, for such a large congregation, isn't the norm. His dedication and love for the Lord inspired many.

Not only was he devoted to the church members; he was even more devoted to his family.

Milt's shining attributes and qualities were all I thought about for a long while. As time passed, I remembered with fondness some of his little quirks that irritated me. I would have given anything to have him back, idiosyncrasies and all. Maybe he wasn't as perfect as I remembered, but he was my beloved. I think it is a part of the grieving process for some to have an unrealistic idea of their loved one at first, but, in time, the memories of the person become realistic.

Facing your regrets, being honest with your wishes, and praying through them, you will be well on your way to healing. Try to face any unfinished business, if it is of concern to you. If your marriage was not what you had hoped for, there must be a different kind of healing brought into your grief-work.

If you have things you would like to say to a deceased loved one, it helps to write a letter. The person is dead; the letter cannot be physically delivered. Regardless, there is a release that comes in setting things down on paper. And, who knows? Maybe the message gets there somehow.

You must grieve, the good, the bad, and the ugly. Perhaps your spouse was struggling with things you were not aware of. Don't sugarcoat his or her faults, but don't dwell on them either. When you get your feelings and fears out in the light, it is easier to let them go.

Ask the Lord to let the shadow of the Cross fall over anything that is wrong. Here the love of God can make things right. Go to the place of ultimate healing and forgiveness. Seek a counselor if you have serious and sensitive issues that won't go away.

Lord Jesus, I put Your Cross in between me and <u>(Name of your loved one)</u>.

I forgive him/her for _____ and _____.
I ask You to heal any unfinished business between us. Please heal any wounds either of us may have caused.

In Jesus' name, I pray.

Workbook – Chapter 7

Because we cannot change the past, we must grieve and let go. The only thing for sure is the love of our Savior Jesus Christ.

❖ Galatians 6:14-NIV
May I never boast except in the cross of our Lord Jesus Christ, through which the world has been crucified to me, and I to the world.

What does the Cross means to you? Healing? Salvation? Other things?

_____
_____
_____

Think of all the facets of it that you can. List them below. Example: Jesus loved you this much. He stretched out His hands and He died.

_____
_____
_____

Think of hymns that contain messages about the Cross, as well as Bible verses. List some here if you wish.

1 Example-When I Survey The Wondrous Cross
2 _____
_____
_____

3 _____

_____

_____

What are some of the words that stir you?

_____

_____

_____

Can you place your spouse or difficult family member beneath the Cross allowing all the pain of the relationship to dissolve in the shadow of it?

_____

_____

_____

The Lord delights to heal and save.

Chapter Eight

Sharing Our Stories, Healing Our Souls

You may be reading this together with a group right now. Perhaps you already have experienced the benefits of sharing your stories. For those readers who haven't been in a support group yet, I would like to share with you the reason other grieving friends can do wonders to help you heal and feel better.

My deepest healing came by helping others with their grief, while at the same time receiving their help for mine. Why does telling our stories heal us? There is something about sharing our pain. Our hurting souls will heal better, just like a wound that is open to light and air has a better chance to heal. When we share from our hearts we open ourselves up to be able to receive the compassion of those who truly understand, building strong bonds. This connectedness will strengthen you at a time when you feel so weak.

Everyone has a story. People need places to tell their stories to others who care. It is a basic human need to "be known," and how else does this happen without sharing our lives? Families used to sit around the fireside and share stories. Grandpa and Grandma would tell about the good old days. Stories knit lives together and build community and a sense of belonging. Real life has bane and blessing, pain and joy. If we become more transparent in our own sharing, it may help others to tell more than their success stories. Revealing your true self is risky. It is even harder for people already in pain.

But if you are grieving a major loss, you especially need to tell the story of the love and relationship you enjoyed with the person who was so much a part of your life. In a support group, you can celebrate the wonder of your loved one, giving you new meaning and hope for the future.

Grief is something we don't want to think about. Our souls need healing and we want it now. Wouldn't it be nice if we could go to a store and buy a jar of Healing Balm of Gilead? I believe that every time we pray with someone about a grief need or ask God for our own healing, that healing balm is applied to our hurts. Healing from any great loss takes time and is a deep work.

Can you relate to "Doubting Thomas?" In John 20:24-28 we see him and it is easy to understand how he felt.

"Now Thomas (called Didymus), one of the Twelve, was not with the disciples when Jesus came. So the other disciples told him, 'We have seen the Lord!'

But he said to them, 'Unless I see the nail marks in his hands and put my finger where the nails were, and put my hand into his side, I will not believe it.'

"A week later his disciples were in the house again, and Thomas was with them. Though the doors were locked, Jesus came and stood among them and said, 'Peace be with you!'

"Then He said to Thomas, 'Put your finger here; see my hands. Reach out your hand and put it into my side. Stop doubting and believe.'

"Thomas said to him, 'My Lord and my God!'"

We mourners can be like Thomas. We so desperately want to come through our experience as fulfilled, happy people. But we just can't see it yet. It seems impossible. Thomas knew that Jesus had died on the cross and he knew his dead body was cold and lying in a grave. He couldn't see how Jesus could possibly have been in the same room, alive. He wasn't there when the others saw Him and he needed proof.

We want proof that God can make this situation of pain and loss come out well, so that we can be happy again. We want life to make sense again. "I love you Jesus, but I hurt and I want your assurance that you have my best interests at heart.

Like Thomas, some of us get mired in our grief and become fearful. We don't want to face our losses. Many people who refuse to face their pain usually dull it in some way instead. This is where addictive behavior comes in. When someone is stuck in grief, encourage him or her to seek Christian counseling. A trusted praying friend is helpful. God will give them what they need to get well.

While I attended my first grief support group, and I had shared my story and listened to some of theirs, I grew strong enough to face a difficult task. I felt it was time to go through Milt's clothes and get them out of the bedroom, to find his personal belongings scattered throughout the house, and make decisions about what to do with everything.

I had no problem putting some of his clothes in plastic sacks and had taken care of that earlier. But some of his personal effects were still in the dresser drawers. It was a milestone to be ready to let go of them. I gave our sons a chance to take some special things as keepsakes. Cleaning out his belongings and setting other things aside to keep, was a way for me to feel as if I was making progress. I knew that if I kept everything as it was, it would be impossible to let go of my "former life." Of course, handling the many cards he gave me, our love letters from our courtship, and his prayer journals, brought on a bout of tears. Some of the things made me smile. It was all part of the process. The question was, "What did I want to keep and what should I let go of?"

I asked my group about this and there were varying degrees of being able to part with things. Their individual personalities entered into their answers. (There is no need to move too quickly on this, only if you are ready.) Many said they kept photos, letters and achievements that their spouses had received. Each person had things that had special meaning for them and items that they decided to recycle or throw away. Some had a hard time doing anything.

Taking off my wedding ring was the hardest thing for me to do. First of all, my fingers had widened and I couldn't pull it off. I had to have it cut off. The symbolism of the deed was heart wrenching. I couldn't stand to leave it off so I had it soldered together and enlarged and kept wearing it. Soon after, I felt it was time to take it off for good. Since I had worn it for so many years, my finger felt naked without it. I have also known of people who never take off their ring after their spouse has died.

Many women make a special new ring out of the gems from the old one in a new setting. Therefore they blend the old as well as something new. This is a great idea. As for me, I eventually had a set of rings from Robert.

I learned that Robert had all of Darlene's (his former wife's) clothes still in his closet when we were planning to sell his house before our marriage. Thankfully, his daughter came to the rescue and went through everything. Not only did she clean out the closet but she went through all the items that he didn't want and had a yard sale. I didn't want to be the one to clear out his memories. Because of the promise of our new life together, he really didn't want to hang on to the clothes, just a few family pictures. He felt uncomfortable dealing with women's clothes. He had no attachment to the furniture and only brought a few things into my house after we were married. This made it easy for me. I heard that it doesn't happen this easily usually and, the other spouse's "baggage" can be a problem.

In sharing stories, we learn from each another. We see that others have the same struggles we do. We can support one another in prayer. A compassionate listener can help to alleviate some pain.

At the end of every session, we took hands and closed with prayer. We prayed for individual struggles in the stories mentioned during the meeting. Then we gave each other warm hugs. Hugs were well appreciated; it is one of the things we miss so much about our spouse. Most grieving people want hugs, but it is important to get their permission first.

I asked some participants about our group, What had helped them the most? These were their responses:

1. I felt free to say how I was feeling with no criticism.
2. It helped to hear others' problems.
3. I got rid of my bitterness when I realized others have losses too.
4. I felt supported even in my depression; "No one said, "You've got to get over it."
5. The listening and caring helped me to feel better.
6. Others' problems were worse than mine, so I stopped feeling alone.
7. I wanted to help the new ones in the group when I began feeling better.

As we shared our stories, we could see how they were healing all of us. Some said they felt so much better, that they didn't need to keep coming. They were ready to move on. Some wanted to channel their new energies into helping the new people just starting the group. A few planned to collect toys and clothing for third world countries. Some helped with teaching and prayer ministries. Doing these things made us feel whole again and caused the body of Christ to grow stronger. My healing continued as I watched their progress.

If you desire to help others, it could be as simple as offering a listening ear to someone. Or it could be as involved as starting a group, as I did.

Here are things to consider if you wish to form a grief support group. How can you make a safe place for people to share? What helps folks open up and tell their heartfelt thoughts so that healing can come?

Trust is so important. We usually don't let our guard down unless we are convinced it is safe to do so. When I was newly widowed, I wanted to talk to people who had experienced what I had. I expected that a group leader would make sure that there would be no criticism between the members, and no unwanted advice. When I found a leader and a group like that, I was relieved. Once I learned to trust them, I felt safe enough to open up to them.

Then, later, as a group leader, my goal for us was to see each person experience more peace now than they had before joining us. My hope was that they would cherish what was good, grieve the loss, and begin to look forward to the future. It was a gift to be able to share their grief. They knew that what they shared with the group would not be repeated outside our circle of friends.

If members of the group didn't feel protected, they wouldn't talk. I was careful not to give advice. It was better to tell what happened to me and share what I had learned. I would explain that my way of handling something was an option, but not the only way. It is unfair to treat vulnerable people as if you knew what was best for them. Had I listened to what the person in my first grief group had suggested, that I turn out my son from home, it would have been disastrous for both of us.

I've led different kinds of small groups for a number of years. Although I have had training in counseling and spiritual guidance, these are not necessary requirements. If you are providing a low-key situation for group sharing, it can be as easy as having people over to your home. My sister formed a group by simply inviting newly widowed coworkers over for dinner. If you are the kind of person who is a good listener and keeps things confidential, it should go well.

In her particular group, there were wonderful break-throughs especially one person who was new in town. She had very few friends and no family for support when her husband died. The group became her lifeline.

Should the person's grief uncover some past problems, one may want to refer them to a formal counselor along with, or instead of, the group. This kind of person could dominate and control the session because of unbearable pain. To prevent this from happening, it is good to have a written covenant that everyone hears and signs in the beginning. (One is available in the first part of the book.) Everyone needs a chance to share, so you, as the facilitator, need to give gentle reminders to keep the discussion moving, without one person using up too much time.

Once you have established precedence, the group will easily abide by what is expected. You need to be gentle but firm about keeping the members on track. Your group won't work if someone dominates or takes up the whole time. But in our group, those who had most recently lost a spouse were given more time to share if they wished.

If a person is working one-on-one with a therapist or spiritual director, they can work on personal issues there. That person may still benefit from the group, but only if he or she will give the others enough time to share. The group can be a big part of healing and I highly recommend having one.

Workbook-Chapter Eight

❖ Psalm 94:17-KJV
Unless the Lord had been my help, my soul had almost dwelt in silence.

Daily the Lord helps us and we do not always recognize it. What has the Lord done in this last week that has helped you cope with your situation?

_____

_____

_____

In the Bible, we have story after story of how God helped His people in times of crisis.

Moses—Parting of the Red Sea—
    ❖ Exodus 14:21—NIV
    Moses stretched out his hand over the sea and all the night the Lord drove back the sea with a strong east wind and turned it to dry land. The waters were divided, and the Israelites went through on dry ground, with a wall of water on their right and on their left.

David—Defeating Goliath—
    ❖ I Samuel 17:45—NIV
    David said to the Philistine, "You come against me with a sword and spear and javelin, but I come against you in the name of the Lord almighty, the God of the armies of Israel, whom you have defied.

Joshua –the battle of Jericho-
❖ Joshua 6:3-NIV
You march around the city once with all the armed men. Do this for six days. Have the priests carry trumpets of rams' horns in front of the ark. On the seventh day, march around the city seven times, with the priests' blowing on the trumpets. When you hear them sound a long blast on the trumpets, have all the people give a loud shout, then the wall of the city will collapse and the people will go up, every man straight in.

We can remember times when God helped us in the past. Please list as many as you can.

Early years _____

_____

_____

Teen years _____

_____

_____

Midlife _____

_____

_____

Later years _____

_____

_____

Chapter 9

How Do I Go On?

My grown children didn't want to see me sad anymore, and perhaps they didn't want to hear about how I felt. They worried that I would never get over my grief. They were happy that I cared so much for their father and that I missed him, but not to the point that I was feeling miserable for such a long time.

> *"Though I walk through the valley of the shadow of death, I will fear no evil, for Thou are with me."*
> *Psalm 23:4 KJV*

"This valley is so dark," I often thought after Milt's death and again after Robert's. I have heard people say that they felt very close to God when a loved one died, but I did not. There are so many phases of missing a person that seem so troublesome. Then I would cry out in my pain and the heaviness would temporarily lift. The loss remained, but the valley began to get brighter eventually.

I knew in my head that God was with me. I just didn't feel His presence very much. Unless I fought against it, a depression cloud stayed with me all day. I couldn't keep it at bay all the time, but kept busy, working hard and doing fun things with friends. Even so, I often felt sad while I was with them.

If I kept my eyes on the Lord by meditating on His promises, instead of my feelings, I'd be better.

Robert and I had planned for two years to go to Europe the summer of 2000. It was going to be a trip of a lifetime — a circle tour of England, France, Brussels, Switzerland, Germany, and Italy. Robert had never been to Europe before and was terribly excited about it.

We had also written a purchase agreement for a town home together and were planning to move there in September. His daughter's wedding was coming up in October. But, he died in April. Our dreams and plans became part of my loss.

I had hard choices to make. After thinking about it, I decided to go on the trip anyway. My sister and her girlfriend were already going. A friend of mine stepped forward and offered to go with me. I knew I would feel sad on the trip, but I thought I would feel worse, if I stayed home. I went, although I grieved during the trip. It was a wonderful time, although much different from what I had envisioned it to be with Robert. Going on that vacation was the right choice for me.

The day we were in Paris, I told my roommate, Carol, that I wished I could dream about Robert. I had known how wonderful it was whenever I had dreamed about Milt. The aching loss I felt for Robert during the trip was dulling my joy. There was a point when our bus passed the Eiffel Tower in Paris that I fell asleep for a short time. I dreamed that Robert was there, walking along beside us on our tour. That was an amazingly kind gift from God.

When I returned home, I closed on the townhouse and moved in. It was hard to do; I felt lonely and cheated. The plan was to live with Robert in that lovely new place. It made me sad to experience my new beginning in my new home, as a widow again. I am thankful that my friends made the difference between terrible and bearable. They helped me move, brought food, and helped me in more ways than they could have known.

I felt close to Robert's family, but grieving him with them was tough. I was not their mother and sometimes felt left out of their circle. It was no one's fault, just the way it was. His daughter's wedding was another difficult day, but I needed to be there. God was with me in all of it.

Embrace your situation, I was told by a friend. I could do that only because I knew I stood in the shadow of the cross. And so I purposed in my heart to accept the hard things that came to me. It was a choice I made, but I could only do so because I stood in the shadow of the cross. In that shadow of Christ's love, I saw how much He suffered for me. When that cross-shaped shadow fell across my losses and my dashed hopes for happiness, what could I say? When I had to "embrace" terribly painful things I simply didn't want to do, I remembered how Jesus embraced the crossbeam and carried it to Golgotha. Like Jesus, I must trust in the Father's good plans for me, and trust that whatever I suffer is in His care.

Making Progress

Over time, I began to feel God's presence more. He helped me cope with individual problems and setbacks so many times. As I have noted, I chose to believe God was with me regardless of how I felt. I talked to the Lord even when I was angry or discouraged. I was brutally honest with Him. Many times, I remembered the Scripture, and said the words to Him: "To whom shall we go? You have the words of eternal life." No, I knew deep down that I could never forsake my trust in God. There is no one like Him. He alone is my help.

During a very dark period, my pastor, a very busy man, asked me to join him in his office once a week so that he could pray for me. He often didn't know what to say to me during our conversations, but his weekly prayers on my behalf were powerfully helpful. They made me feel like I was a valuable part of the Body of Christ. I am so thankful that he didn't give me platitudes. With confidence in God, he knew the Holy Spirit would comfort me.

I believe faith and hope is what helped me to go on. I knew my departed loved ones were safe and at peace and that I would see them some day.

With God's help, I focused on how much I still had to live for; my family on earth still needed me. I could help my grown children and grandchildren; I had gifts and callings on my life, things to do that no one else could do. I found it good to say things to myself like, "I will go on." "I can make it through." "I can do all things through Christ who strengthens me." Other times, it seemed too hard. I took one step through the valley and then another one. That's all I could do.

Make plans. There is so little time in life. We can submit our plans to God and He will bring them to pass, or He will make corrections along the way. His plans are for our good and to trust in this truth is freeing.

When you start making plans after getting past the initial shock of the death of your loved one, you then know you are on the way to healing. Making new plans and finding things to live for will empower you. If you expectantly seek God and ask Him to show you the way you should go, He will give you direction. He wants you to live in hope.

Depression is like a weedy garden; we need to tend to it. We must pull all the weeds out of it that we can. The weeds are negative thoughts. "I can't live without my spouse. Life isn't worth living." You know the kind. Counterattack them with God's word. Then let the gentle rain of Jesus and the sunshine of His love do their work. No one ever said it would be easy, just like weeding is hard, consistent work.

If you have had a history of depression, you already may have helpers in process, i.e. therapist, medication. For many bereaved, the depression is a next-to-the last stage or task of grieving. Knowing that can be helpful. Surround yourself with compassionate, positive people. It is great to have someone who believes in you. To this person you can be honest when they say something that is not helpful. They should be willing to listen and learn from you. There is a benefit for both of you.

Affirming your faith can help. 2 Corinthians 4:8 NIV says it all: — "We are hard pressed on every side, but not crushed; perplexed, but not in despair, persecuted, but not abandoned: struck down, but not destroyed. This verse talks about fighting the enemy against his discouragement and opposition. We may feel destroyed but the truth is, we cannot be defeated if we trust in God."

Don't listen to "Job's friends." (Sometimes we can be like "Job's friends" to ourselves.) These people say things like, "it won't get better." "The second year is harder." Those things are not true necessarily. Say out loud, "It will get better."

How do you move on to the healing place? Even if you don't like writing, I suggest journaling. It helps to see progress in the written record of your journey. I suggest writing without worrying if you will offend anyone in the slim chance your journal is read some day. You can always throw it away when you are ready. Don't worry about your penmanship. Don't fret about grammar. Write from the heart quickly, freely, openly, getting all you are feeling out into the light. You can always put a "disclaimer" on the beginning—"This writing is written in the depth of grieving; please understand that my emotions are raw.

Another helpful thing to do is to share your progress with a discerning friend. Can you see a shift or growth from the early weeks to now? Another person may observe things that seem unimportant. Sometimes we're too close to our own situations to see the truth.

Congratulate yourself on how far you have come. Celebrate small victories. Know that you will have setbacks in that you think you're returning to where you were six months ago. But it isn't true. You are making progress, though it may not always seem like it.

I had an open house for the friends who helped me after Milt's death. I called it –"Thanks for helping me get through the first year party." The idea came to me as I was dreading the first anniversary of his death. It turned my focus of loss to a reason to celebrate. As I prepared for the party, I realized how good it was to keep busy all day. The event helped my friends to see how important their help had been to me. I truly was thankful for their kindness. All I needed to do was make a few goodies and clean the house.

Since I love being with people, it helped me. I know there are many who wouldn't want to do such a thing. But there are other ways to remember your loved ones' life.

The hospital Milt died in had a Memorial Service for the survivors of those who had died a year ago. My sister's husband was in hospice before he died. They planned a memorial service for the loved ones of deceased hospice patients and held it right before Christmas. We lit a candle for those who had died and put it on a wooden "tree." These things were all meaningful. It can be just a quiet memorial in your home, alone, or with a few friends. It can be a wonderful way to remember and also to see that you've come such a long way.

The time comes when we must really say goodbye. We must let them go, not out of our memories and hearts, but in our need for them. Time to take off the ring he gave you; time to put away the clothes, and the trophies. It is time to realize that love goes on forever, but there is a time to say farewell and give them to God. You and God will be the ones to decide when that will be.

Workbook - Chapter Nine

❖ I Pet. 2:6- NIV
See, I lay in Zion, a chosen and precious cornerstone, and the one who trusts in Him will never be put to shame.

If this promise is true, what is the most important task I have?

❖ I Pet. 2:9-NIV
But you are a chosen people, royal priests, a holy nation, a people belonging to God that you may declare the praises of Him who called you out of darkness into his wonderful light. Once you were not a people, but now you are the people of God; once you had not received mercy, but now you have received mercy.

Chosen! You and I have been chosen to tell others about the wonderful acts of God. What a great thing, to be called out of darkness to receive God's mercy.

Think some of God's actions in your life. In what specific ways have you experienced His light? Then find someone you can share these with. List them here if you wish.

In what way can our telling the "good news" be a memorial to your deceased loved one?
The best way to do this is to tell others what God has done for you.

_____

_____

_____

Name the people in your life who have helped you desire to "go on."

_____

_____

_____

Thank them by writing them a note or calling them on the telephone.

Chapter 10

What is my Reason for Living? What is my Passion?

I always knew my reason for living wasn't my husband. I had many other interests outside of my home. I was in retreat ministry, and I had continued formal education. My life apart from Milt's was an extremely fulfilling one. However, he was such an integral part of my life that when he suddenly taken from me, everything seems to fall apart. Life for me at that moment was like Jenga, the tower game of little rectangular wooden blocks that start out all neatly stacked. You can remove blocks little by little from the top and sides and even in the middle of the tower, but when a "key" block is removed, the tower topples. After his death, I felt like a bunch of blocks lying on the ground.

God cares much more than we know about our grief. Here are a couple of illustrations that reveal His heart.

In the raising of Lazarus, we see His concern quite dramatically. First of all, Jesus doesn't view death as heavily as we do; He knows it is not an end but a new beginning in eternity. However, in Lazarus's case, Jesus wanted to show the world that He had power of life over death. It was a grievous lesson for those in Bethany until He arrived. When He saw Mary's tears, and those of the ones with her, He was deeply moved and began to weep too. His tears weren't for Lazarus, and his sorrow wasn't about losing His friend—his tears were for Mary and Martha, and their friends, and for all of us who have lost our loved ones.

God's heart hasn't changed. As the author of our lives, He knows the end from the beginning:

"For I know the plans I have for you," declares the Lord, "plans to prosper you and not to harm you, plans to give you hope and a future" (Jeremiah 29:11). This message had been sent to the exiled nation of Israel after their captivity.

God wants us to be happy and to live passionately and with purpose. How do we go from captivity to freedom?

God wants us to live out of the desires of our hearts. He cares about our dreams and our setbacks. He has put all of our hopes and dreams for fulfillment inside of us. We were created with certain interests, skills, and talent. Our love for Him will actually stir these things up and become part of our direction and purpose. This is what is meant by passion, in a spiritual sense. We can feel passionate about God when we cross the line from knowing *about* Him to knowing *Him*. Intimacy with God comes with daily walking with Him, from talking and listening to Him.

Only God can heal us and take us into His plans and purposes He has in mind for us.

I believe I was like the woman with the issue of blood in Mark 5:25-30. A large crowd followed and pressed around Jesus. A sickly woman was there and had been subject to bleeding for twelve years. She had suffered a great deal under the care of doctors and had spent all her money to get well, yet instead of getting better she grew worse. When she heard about Jesus, and saw Him in the crowd, she squeezed through the people and touched his cloak. She believed, "If I just touch his clothes, I will be healed."

Immediately the bleeding stopped and she felt in her body that she was freed from her suffering. At once Jesus realized that power had gone out form him. He turned around in the crowd and asked, "Who touched Me?"

Like her, I was weary of crying, sighing and hurting. I didn't have a disease, but at times people acted as if widowhood was an illness. The woman in the story was literally drained and at her wits end. She believed that if she touched the edge of Jesus' robe, she could be healed.

Eventually I was healed, not by the "doctors" in my life, but by Jesus. When I continued to pray, even though I was angry, when I was honest with Him about my feelings, when I persisted in asking, seeking and knocking, Jesus answered my prayers. I got to know Him in the darker parts of my life in a deeper way than in the lighter times. He healed me and brought into a deeper relationship with Himself.

Just like the woman in the Bible, I will not keep silent about what He has done for me.

If you are still devastated from your loss, you might not be ready to think about the future. But when you are ready, you will want to share what God has done for you.

You can heal. You can feel better. Life can be good again. I say this again, because we grieving people have a hard time with believing it. I know happiness will come into your life again.

What is your passion? Follow your heart. What do you just love to do and can concentrate on? If you find something meaningful to do, you'll hardly notice that time has passed. I have mentioned some things that others have done in earlier chapters.

It made me angry when people told me, "Now you can write, as you have wanted to for years. It seemed like a trade-off—Milt's death in exchange for my writing. When I finally realized that writing wasn't a trade-off, but that it was a passion God had lit in my heart, I knew it was time to do it. Just as I have done ever since I gave my life to Christ,

I prayed about what to write about. I asked Him to give me words. Writing is hard work but it is part of my love for Him and the passion He's given me.

God wants us to live abundantly and passionately. Healing from grief is a journey from barely surviving to living passionately.

How do you get back on track and live the life God has planned for you? Your circumstances have changed, but you are still you. Actually, your life isn't really off track, it just feels that way. Your journey through this dark valley hasn't taken you off course. You can only go off course if you give up the journey of faith.

So, what would you like to do that you might really enjoy? Arise, take God's hand and do something meaningful with Him.

I found that helping others was at the top of my list. If I am playing with or teaching children, talking to elderly, assisting some one with an errand, or caring for someone sick, I am filled with joy. The happiest people I know are those with their focus outward, away from themselves.

Volunteer positions are numerous. Many are needed in churches and hospitals and other places. If you don't have a lot of family nearby, "adopt" a grandchild, grandparent, or person of another culture. In our town, many refugees are coming in and need much help adjusting to our country. I adopted a refugee family—a single mom and her children. Her friendship has so enriched my life.

What skills do you have or need to sharpen? What kinds of things interest you? You could take a course in computers, photography, pottery, cake decorating, or organizing closets. There are countless possibilities.

If you have to work to earn a living, this can be a blessing. God knows your situation. Sometimes, new skills are needed for a better job. Even though new things can be scary, just remember, God has every one of your days written in the book of your life. As your life's author, you can trust that He will carry you through every hardship, every frightening challenge, and He will make only good come out of your situations. He is with you. Look for Him in every day; notice His help and compassion. He wants you to live a fulfilling and meaningful life.

Perhaps you need new friends. You are in a new time now.

Making new friends at a Christian singles group really helped me out. They were flexible and open to try new activities, more than my married friends.

Some people in my singles group are interested in finding a new spouse, or at least someone to have a relationship with. Just be sure you don't rush into a relationship to fill the empty space. Your new friend cannot take the place of your loved one, if you try to make this happen, it will end in more pain. Take time to grieve, as much is right for you. If you are willing to feel the pain now, then if someone special comes along you will be ready for a new partner.

We can trust in God's good plans for us. Milt and Robert were my love-partners, two important characters in the story-plot of my life. Obviously, they were in different chapters, but they were part of one story. God has been writing the book of my life before I was born. Milt's death came as no surprise to God, nor did Robert's.

The morning Milt died, he wrote things in his journal that were more than coincidental; his prayer time was part of his intimate relationship with the Lord.

II Cor.4:18- "Good news! The troubles will soon be over, but the joys to come will last forever."
Alleluia!

II Cor. 5:6-Therefore we are always confident, knowing that while we are at home in the body, we are absent from the Lord.
"What a super attitude. We look forward to our heavenly bodies, realizing that every moment we spend in our earthly bodies is time spent away from our eternal home in heaven with Jesus."

That day, Milt left his earthly body and looked into the loving eyes of Jesus.

During his morning devotions, the Scriptures he read were about this life being temporary.

2 Cor.4:17-18 says this: "For our light affliction, which is but for a moment, is working for us a far more exceeding and eternal weight of glory, while we do not look at the things which are seen, but at the things which are not seen. For the things which are seen are temporary, but the things which are not seen are eternal."

My husband rejoiced that morning and God rejoiced with him.

This text was written in Milt's funeral brochure:

2 Timothy 4,6b,7,8 —
"The time is here for me to leave this life. I have done my best in the race. I have run the full distance, and I have kept the faith. And now there is waiting for me the prize of victory awarded for a righteous life, the prize which the Lord, the righteous Judge, will give me on that Day, and not only to me, but to all who wait with love for him to appear."

Did Milt know? I've wondered. What I know for sure is that Milt's life and his death were precious to Jesus.

"Precious in the sight of the Lord is the death of His saints" (Psalm 116:15).

The Blessed Hope

In the beginning of this book I mentioned how, when suddenly my world fell apart, I cried out to God, "Where is my hope now?"

His answers have brought us to the conclusion of this book.

My hope is based solely on the all-powerful, all-knowing love of God. *He* is my only hope. He has brought me on a painful journey to healing and wholeness. I would not be the person I am today had I not traveled this unwanted path.

I know the love of God and the power of God, more than I did before my grief.

I believe the words "I trust you" means more to Jesus than "I love you." To say, "I trust you," no matter what is happening, captures His heart. This is what moves Him.

I cling to Jesus' cloak, willing myself to be healed, and He raises me up, holds me close and whispers, "Everything is going to be all right."

He sees the end of all sorrow and the beginning of unimaginable joy.

Brennan Manning says it this way, "In the end everything will be all right. Nothing can harm you permanently; no loss is lasting, no defeat more than transitory, no disappointment is conclusive. Suffering, failure, loneliness, sorrow, discouragement, and death will be part of your journey, but the kingdom of God will conquer all these horrors." Amen!

Who knows how many days are allotted to me and what else will come my way? Only God knows, and I have learned to trust Him. So, I live each day with all the zeal and hope that is in me.

When suddenly my world fell apart, God painstakingly put it back together. Praise to Him who gives me victory through Jesus Christ.

I bless each of you who have read this book. My prayer for you is that you will discover the depths of God's tender heart towards you, and that the joy of Jesus will live in you.

Workbook – Chapter 10

What is my passion? What is my reason for living?

_____

_____

_____

❖ I Peter 4:10
As each has received a gift, minister it to one another,
as good stewards of the manifold grace of God.

Why has God given us these gifts?

_____

_____

_____

List your gifts and how you have used them lately. (Little things count, like listening to a friend, helping someone with a task.)

What motivates you to minister to others?

How does the preciousness of life impact your serving others?

_____

_____

_____

Read Psalm 139 with the Lord. Let the reality of that Psalm fill you. Write any thoughts.

_____

_____

_____

What is your life's Mission Statement? Are you living it right now? If not, in what way would you like to? Have you ever written one? If not, do it now and ask the Lord to show you, specifically, what it is. Write it here. God bless you.

Recommended Reading

In my search for helpful books on grief for my own healing, as well as material to use as a grief support leader and counselor, the following books I recommend:

* Life is Goodbye, Life is Hello: Grieving Well Through All kinds of Loss, by Alla Renee Bozarth Hazelden, Hazelden Publishing

  Alla Bozarth is an Episcopal priest and psychotherapist who talks about attitudes toward grief of all kinds. She gives a comprehensive study of life changes that cause it and practical help in overcoming grief. "We become agents in our own healing process, instead of victims of our grief." Poetry reinforces this work.

* Praying Your Goodbyes by Joyce Rupp, OSM, Ave Maria Press
  Joyce Rupp shares her own losses through death and other life changes. There is need for closure with all kinds of loss. She composes rituals that give can give meaning to these "goodbyes" that often are not acknowledged. She asserts that there is freedom and healing in letting go.

❖ God in the Dark—Through Grief and Beyond by Luci Shaw, Zondervan
Luci Shaw shares her thoughts recorded from her journal during her journey with the terminal cancer and eventual death of Harold Shaw, her beloved husband. With great honesty, she tells of the dark night of God when she could not see Him clearly. She also shares about other times when His illuminating light brought hope.

❖ My Companion Through Grief –Comfort For Your Darkest Hours by Gary Kinnaman, Regal- (Gospel Light) Gary has arranged topics surrounding grief in short companion pieces so that those who are heart sore and cannot bear to read too much can start with short bits to encourage their souls. Excellently done and covers all types of grief.

❖ How to Handle Grief: Tracks of a fellow struggler by John Claypool, Word Publishing. This is a good study for those who have asked such questions as "Does God Care?" and the big one,"Why?"

❖ When Men Grieve-Why men grieve differently and how you can help by Elizabeth Levang, PhD, Fairview Press. These are personal stories and commentary in an easy-to-read format. Very helpful for men who are grieving, and for those who love them. Will lead you to a deeper understanding of men and how they process things. It's good!

❖ Let Me Grieve But Not Forever-by Verdell Davis, Word Publishing. The book is taken from the journals of Davis' journals. Well written, lots of parallels for me because her late husband was also a minister.

CPSIA information can be obtained at www.ICGtesting.com
Printed in the USA
266672BV00001B/4/A

9 781600 349089